TRINITY

An Impediment to Christ (Messiah)

KA-SERVANT OF CHRIST

A wake up call for the chosen ones to have faith
in Christ's teachings instead of man's

TRINITY
AN IMPEDIMENT TO CHRIST (MESSIAH)

Scripture taken from the New King James Version®. Copyright © 1982 by Thomas Nelson. Used by permission. All rights reserved.

iUniverse books may be ordered through booksellers or by contacting:

iUniverse
1663 Liberty Drive
Bloomington, IN 47403
www.iuniverse.com
1-800-Authors (1-800-288-4677)

ISBN: 978-1-5320-2579-2 (sc)
ISBN: 978-1-5320-2580-8 (e)

Library of Congress Control Number: 2017909064

Print information available on the last page.

iUniverse rev. date: 02/18/2020

CONTENTS

ACKNOWLEDGMENTS

First of all, I am very thankful to God and His Christ who gave me the wisdom and the revelation to connect the old scriptures to the New Testament. This blessing has allowed me to zoom in on the truth, in the scriptures, to expose the fabricated doctrine of trinity. Secondly, I would like to thank my wife and my children who have filled my life with joy and happiness. Last, but not least, I am also thankful to my mother who has raised me as a single parent.

PART ONE

ABOUT THE AUTHOR AND THE HISTORY OF TRINITY

CHAPTER 1
A BIOGRAPHICAL NOTE

I was born in Aram, the land where Christ feet touched and where He taught. I am by no means sinless, but I have been given the wisdom to tie the New Testament to the old and see and hear it clearly. The doctrine of trinity beclouded my thinking and render me irreligious when I was young. The doctrine of trinity did not dovetail with the New Testament or the old scriptures. Later in life the Spirit took control of my life and I began to dream of things yet to occur. These dreams took me all the way to Egypt where I married my Christian wife and I began to be drawn like a magnet to the bible.

I began to rewind the hands of time to the true teachings of Christ. Notwithstanding that I spent 4 years in the seminary, I do not consider myself a theologian; I am an engineer. I feel that God has touched me to wake up the chosen ones and correct the teachings. The return of God's only begotten Son, Christ, is in the offing. The Holy Spirit took control of my life few years back and drove me to write this book to raise the awareness of the faithful before the end of times. God is a jealous God and He does not want us to worship anyone but Him. God, Himself, buried Moses to make sure that the men of Israel do not worship him (Deuteronomy 34:5-7). I know that some will not like this book, but I am not here to please man; I am here to please God as stated in 1 Thessalonians 2:4. I am not affiliated with any church or any Christian denomination. This book is not asking the reader to switch denominations, but rather invoking a wake-up call before it is too late. This book is written to, merely, raise your awareness of the truth and the scriptures. The trinity is the root cause of the burgeoning of the numerous denominations. This book contains only scriptures and history; it does not contain any of my opinions because I cannot pass a judgment against anyone. My opinion cannot save you; however, the scriptures can save you. What it boils down to is that whether you are following the scriptures (old and new) or not because the scriptures contain divine conveyance and not human irreverence. Some people will argue that, without the trinity, Christ has no heavenly value. Using this faulty logic, I can surmise also that none of the prophets, to include Moses, have any heavenly or biblical values either. If the Holy books do not mention a divine conveyance or a doctrine, then you should refrain from following it because it is a man created doctrine identical to idolatry era of the antiquity.

CHAPTER 2

THE HISTORY OF TRINITY

If a doctrine is not cited in the Holy books, then it should not be pronounced by your mouth or followed in your heart. Doing away with trinity does not do away with Christ; on the contrary, it magnifies and solidifies Christ's teachings and purpose as a savior. God does not die; it is a blasphemy to believe that God died to please man. **If Christ did not preach the trinity and the apostles did not convey it, then invoking the trinity is an insult to God and His Christ**. Not once, Christ has talked about the trinity and not once the apostles preached it. **Trinity came into existence in the fourth century, centuries long after Christ and the apostles have gone.** This book will show you how trinity detracts from Christ's teachings and blasphemes against God and insults Christ. **Trinity is a rebellion and rejection of God's instructions.** The New Testament labeled Christ as the Son of man or Son of God 256 times and for the council of nicea to change that doctrine and preach a different gospel is truly a rebellion's against God's word that passed to us thru Christ. In Numbers 23:19, the old scriptures clearly stated that God is not man or a son of man to relent or lie. One cannot find favor in God's eyes by rejecting what Christ instructed us to do. **In 1 Samuel chapter**

15, the old scriptures stated that God is not a man to relent or change His mind. How can the follower considers himself faithful by heeding a human doctrine and rejecting Christ teaching? The New Testament stated that Christ is the Son of God. **Not once Christ said that He is God as God of Israel has repeated many times in the old scriptures. Not once Christ instructed us to worship Him, but rather directed us to pray and worship the Father who is a spirit as stated in John 4:24.** The New Testament, in Hebrews 1:4, states that **Christ was made or became better than the angels. God is not made and does not change status; it is a blasphemy to say that God is made. This blasphemy can put you in the crosshair of an eternal damnation (Mark 3:29).**

The only faith one needs to have is to believe that Christ is the Messiah, Son of God, our savior and that God has raised Him from the dead (Romans 10:9). I am writing this book to wake up the chosen ones and to correct the teachings of Christianity. This manuscript tackles the error promulgated by the Council of Nicea. The Council of Nicea has branched off from the original teachings of Christ and the apostles. The doctrine of trinity caused an error in the Christian faith from which other denominations have burgeoned and created a convoluted Christianity.

Some Christian scholars want to disassociate Islam from Christianity, but the facts point to the association. The fact of the matter is that Islam is the result of Christianity. If ones does some theological research, one will get the same fact. The New Testament was written in the first century. The Roman empire did not understand or cared for the Jewish monotheistic religion (they thought of them as heretics); however, with Christ's miracles and power, it introduced a totally confounding understanding for the Roman empire and it began to give the impression of a religion that they can understand (multiple

4

gods). However, the Roman empire could not perceive the nature of Christ. In the 4th century, the emperor Constantine I, a neophyte, wanted the bishops to discourse the nature of Christ. Constantine I was a pagan and worshipped the sun god "Sol Invictus". The sun was an important god during the Roman empire and they have inscribed it on their currency. The Council of Nicea, made up of its bishops, was formed with the emperor as the presiding official or a "judge". The discourse took place between two parties; on one side they were the Christians who advocated for what has been passed by the Apostles and the other party was in favor of changing the gospel to a Trinitarian based religion. The "Trinitarian" party found favor in the eyes of the 'judge" and the council declared a new doctrine that Christ is also God. The main figure that defended the doctrine of trinity was not even a priest; he was a deacon. This deacon, who defended the doctrine of trinity against the other priests, came from parents who worshipped idols and multiple gods. However, according to history, this defender of the trinity turned to Christianity. The idea of trinity was finalized by the Council of Nicea under this emperor and was put on solid ground by the emperor Theodosius. Theodosius made it a crime for anyone to preach Christianity without the Trinity doctrine. The Roman empire labeled the true followers of Christ and the Jews as "heretics". Two emperors with no theological knowledge have shaped the Christian religion because trinity was an acceptable idea at that time.

The Romans had 12 Gods. They can relate to the trinity idea of the Greeks who had Zeus, Poseidon and Aidoneus; the Indians had Brahma, Vishnu, and Shiva; the ancient Egyptians had Amun, Ptah, and Re. The Babylonians had their trinity; baal, ishtar and tammuz. The old scriptures, in Ezekiel 8:13-14, it discussed this type of divine worship and God's disdain of it. All the religions of antiquities had their own divine trinities. The origin of this doctrine is entirely pagan.

The ancient Egyptians had the most influence on this trinity doctrine; they arranged their gods in trinities. For example, Osiris, Isis, Horus; the trinity of Amen, Mut, and Khonsu; the trinity of Satis, Khnum and Anukis etc. This doctrine suited the emperor Constantine I and as such he instituted it with the help of Christ betrayers that the churches venerated as saints. Constantine I was a true pagan who worshipped the sun and he considered the sun god as the main god that explains other wizardry. **Is it coincidental that the churches, to-date, use the sun as an explanation for the trinity doctrine?** The reason the doctrine of trinity prevailed and credit was given to the defenders of this fake doctrine is because the idea of trinity suited the Roman empire which fully endorsed it. The doctrine of the trinity has no biblical basis. It has caused some Christian people to lose faith and caused people of other faiths to steer clear from Christianity (gave the impression of a religion that violates monotheism) where they could have converted to Christianity. **The trinity is truly an impediment to Christ's teachings and Christianity in general.** Christ was sent to earth by the Father to save the world and not just Christians. The Epistle of 1 John 5:7 clearly states that the Father, Word, and Holy Spirit are the same entity in heaven. Father is synonymous with God; God is a Holy Spirit, and since God appeared to prophets by projecting His Words, He is also referred to as the Word. Christ is not mentioned anywhere in this declaration.

Arius the priest was the main figure from Alexandria, Egypt, who fought against the trinity doctrine. Arius declared that this newly created doctrine is in violation of Christ's teachings and the New Testament that was passed by the Apostles. From the beginning, the Christians were under a lot of pressure, from the Roman empire, to change the gospel to make it based on a Trinitarian doctrine to dovetail it with their belief. As a matter of fact, Paul, the apostle, has spoken of this gospel changing and preaching in Galatians 1:6. The supporters of the Council of Nicea, along with the Roman empire, persecuted Arius and his followers.. In the meantime, one of Arius followers, named Bahira, met Muhammad as a child in Basra Syria. Bahira vowed to fight back. According to history, Bahira saw prophetic evidence in Muhammad and became Muhammad teacher. However, as Muhammad grew, he adopted his own teachings and admissions. Other writers contributed to their book and one of these writers were Osman Ibn Affan and others.

This is clear from the Quran in (Surah 21:26) where it states that God has taken up a Son. ISA (Christ in Arabic) is the Son of God.

Arius proclaimed that Christ is **not** God, but the **son of God** as clearly stated in the New Testament. Christ, Himself, has attested many times, in the New Testament, that indeed He is not God, but was sent by God. If Christ is God, He would have said, that "He came to earth" and not "sent to earth". The council of Nicea, by preaching and violating what is written in the New Testament, received the curse that Paul discussed in Galatians 1:8. Again, Paul the apostle hinted to this gospel changing and preaching in Galatians 1:6. Here is a question to ponder: **what gospel was Paul, the apostle, referring to in Galatians 1:6?** There was no other gospel than what the apostles have preached. The only change, in gospel preaching, was the preaching of this multi-gods or the Trinitarian doctrine that the Council of Nicea, finally, proclaimed.

Rome was divided into 4 regions. Constantine's dying father ruled the west. The Eastern part was ruled by emperor Maxentius and emperor Constantine I ruled over the middle-east areas to include Constantinople (turkey today). Constantine wanted to consolidate all Rome under him; however, there was one problem. This problem stemmed from the fact that some roman soldiers and roman elites were practicing Christianity. The majority of Rome practiced paganism and during that time, there was a secretive roman religious cult that followed the god mithras. That cult has ideologies that resembled the Christian religion. Constantine devised a ploy to infuse this pagan religion into Christianity. He proclaimed that he saw a vision of the cross and wanted to become a Christian. After the battle of the Milvian bridge on 28 October 312, Constantine being the victor over emperor Maxentius, he decided to invite 1800 bishops to discuss the nature of Christ. Only 318 bishops showed up and some deacons accompanied these bishops. The remainder bishops did not oblige the pagan emperor because they knew it was a way to change the teaching of the Apostles. That small representation (approx. 18%), by itself, should tell the reader that Constantine was NOT interested into Christianity at all; otherwise, he should have the concurrence of as much bishops as possible. The emperor did not care whether these bishops agreed or not; he had one vision in mind; to change Christianity forever. He wanted to solidify and infuse the pagan ideas into Christianity with or without the rest of the bishops. This emperor knew that he will force this new doctrine on the rest of Christians using his power. Again trinity is the basic deity element of the idol worshippers.

One very influential bishop was present during the Council of Nicea; his name was Eusebius of Nicomedia. Like Arius, Eusebius was a pupil of Lucian of Antioch, so it was natural to support Arius in the Council of Nicea debate. This bishop favored the side of Arius stating that Christ is NOT God but the Son of God holding firm to the teaching of the Apostles and the scriptures. The initial tally between the Arians and non-Arians were evenly split. Eusebius vote angered Constantine and he struck a deal with Eusebius to change his vote in favor of the Non-Arians with a promise to make him famous by allowing him to baptize the emperor Cosntantine. History states that Eusebius convinced others to do the same. History tells us that Eusebius changed his vote and signed the proclamation in favor of the non-Arians; however, history also states that Eusebius signed that declaration with ink but not with heart.

The main deacon, Athanasius, a man who came from an idol worshipping parents, was the main proponents of the proclamation in support of the non-Arian stance. As a matter of fact, Constantine labeled this deacon, a "man of God". A pagan worshipping emperor labeled Athanasius a "man of God". Maybe it should have been written as a "man of one of the gods". This deacon was venerated as a saint in the churches who adopted this fake doctrine of trinity. For further details, one can do history or theology research on Constantine I, Eusebius of Nicomedia and Athanasius by looking at their history. The History Channel has done a segment on Constantine. This episode can be viewed on you-tube under the title of "the deception of Constantine". It can be viewed by visiting https://www.youtube.com/watch?v=TY1_sYnr0gE.

Everyone who follows his/her religion will tell you that theirs is the correct religion. This assertion is no different for the Christians who are following their churches that are garbed in this man made "trinity" doctrine. The trinity doctrine meshes neither with the old scriptures nor with the New Testament. The New Testament must fulfill the old scriptures. The trinity doctrine beclouds and hinders that fulfillment as the later chapters, in this book, will reveal. The followers are tailing the blind leaders at their own perils. Christ was not sent to earth to make His teachings hard to understand or confusing; Christ wanted salvation for all. Christ instructed us, in Matthew 23:8, that we should not be called teachers, because our teacher is one, and that is Himself, Christ. This declaration reverberates the ironclad evidence that all should be obvious and understandable. Nowhere, in the old scriptures, it says that the Messiah is God. As a matter of fact, in Isiah 53, it talked about the Messiah as a **servant** who will suffer and carry our sorrows. The New Testament reminded us of this declaration in Matthew 12:18. The New Testament, factually, reconfirmed this statement by the suffering and crucifixion of Christ. Additionally, the old scriptures in Isaiah 42 and 53 state that **God will put His Spirit on this servant**. The New Testament reconfirms this fact in Acts 10:38 where it is states that God anointed Christ with the Holy Spirit and power. The New Testament was very clear to state that Christ is the Son of God over and over, the Messiah, or the anointed one as the Jewish scriptures stated. Christ, Himself, has taught these scriptures in the synagogues. The old scriptures and the New Testament must go hand in hand to understand God and His Christ. Christ has said, in Mathew 5:18, that till heaven and earth pass away, not one dot, nor one title pass from the law till all is fulfilled. We cannot start a new religion and ignore Christ teachings by doing away with the old scriptures. God is the same in the past, present and the future.

The New Testament was written in Greek and the initial translation stated that Christ was the Messiah, the son of God, or the anointed one. Nowhere, in the original New Testament, it stated that Christ was God, until the churches began to sporadically and slyly inserting that idea in the gospels. These insertions were made to defend the decree that the council of Nicea came up with. The churches began to distance Christ from His Jewish identity (even though the bible clearly stated it). The churches began inserting the word "God' sporadically in the New Testament to reference Christ. Currently, there are approximately 26 versions of the bible.

Here is an ironclad evidence of this sly insertion; note the insertion of the word "God" in the gospel of John 1:18 to state that Christ is God. This insertion was made in the New American Standard Bible and some other bibles, whereas in King James version, it states that Christ is in the bosom of God. This insertion is not limited to John 1:18. The word "God" was sporadically inserted in other areas. Also, note how, in Mathew 24:36, some versions (New King James, Jubilee, NET) omitted the word "Son" from that sentence to solidify the idea of trinity. Whereas, the rest of the versions correctly left the word "Son". Note that in Mathew 24:36 and in Mark 13:32, the New Testament states that the end of time (day and hour), no one knows, not even the angels of heaven, **nor the Son**, but the Father. By omitting the word "Son", the churches slyly diffused any dichotomies arising therefrom. Otherwise, the faithful will quickly realize that the Son cannot be God or the Father since He does not know what the Father knows.

The churches, following the Council of Nicea doctrine, began to interpret their own ways and began to run into dichotomies because the doctrine passed by the Council was in error and could not reconcile with the rest of what is written in the New Testament and the old scriptures. The churches began to tell their congregations to just have faith and believe. Having faith in God's doctrine is one thing and having faith in man's doctrine is another. As a result of all the different interpretations, that are caused by the doctrine of trinity, the churches could not agree among themselves as to how to address this new doctrine and what fell from it. Consequently, multiple denominations burgeoned.

The only place in the bible where they have inserted the trinity idea is in Matthew 28:19. Even though, it vaguely alludes to the trinity, it did not bluntly call it as one. However, the evidences that refute the trinity in the New Testament and the old scriptures way surpass that doctrine. They either were blinded by God or did not want to make serious changes to the New Testament.

In Luke 6:46, Christ uttered "...why you call me Lord and not follow my teaching...?" Christ knew that the day of judgment will come, but He warned us about what is going to happen in Matthew 7:21-23.

I often wonder what happened to the 10 commandments. Christ did not tell us to let go of it or delete some of it. He told us that He did not come to abolish the old scriptures as stated in Matthew 5:17. As matter of fact, when one asked Christ as to what to do to get eternal life, Christ told him to follow the commandments as explained in Luke 18:20.

Human beings understand in only one of two ways; **inferential reasoning and non-deductive reasoning**. The first is based on implicit statements whereas the latter is based on explicit statements. The first uses subjectivity whereas the latter objectivity. If one says the plate is damaged; one can say, the edges are chipped, another can say it is whole but has a crack in it, yet another can say it is broken into 2 pieces and all of these three can defend their viewpoints (but they cannot all be correct). However, if one says the plate is broken into 2 pieces and as such it is damaged; subjectivity is taken out. The majority of the current Christian teachings are based on inferential reasoning and rebellion against the explicit statements cited in the bible. When Christ Himself said in the book of Revelation, Chapter 3:12, "...he who overcomes, I will make him a pillar in the temple of My God..." then it is over, no more guessing is allowed; the truth has been revealed. We cannot take man's opinion and interpretation over Christ and follow it by dubbing these people saints especially where their doctrine contradicts Christ. In 1 Corinthians 11:3, it says that the head of every man is Christ and the head of a woman is man, and the head of Christ is God. Should we then invoke subjectivity and say since Christ is God, then a man is a woman using this logic?

We must adhere to what is written in the gospel because Christ trampled death thru the gospel as stated in 2 Timothy 1:10. Deceivers will convince you otherwise invoking traditions as discerned in Colossians 2:8, but remember that satan can also transform into an angel of light as stated in 2 Corinthians 11: 14. Why Christ chastised the Pharisees, Sadducees and the scribes? Did He chastise them because they followed the scriptures? on the contrary, He did it because they did not, they rebelled and replaced God's Words with traditions and teachings of the elders (Mark 7:13). I see that history is repeating itself. The doctrine that Christ passed to us is God's and not His as written in John 7:16 and John 12:49 because God anointed Him and was with Him (Acts 10:38). One Having God with Him is different than being God. However, what is written in the gospel does not diminish from Christ place in heaven. Notwithstanding that God is boundless, Christ sits at the right hand of God interceding on our behalf (Romans 8:34) and through Whom are all things (1 Corinthians 8:6). Christ did not come to earth to lie and deceive us. It is man who changed the facts and perverted the gospel of Christ by teaching a different Jesus and a different gospel as alluded to in Galatians 1:6, 2 Corinthians 11: 4. As matter of fact, in 1 John 4:15, it says "whoever confesses that Christ is the Son of God, God abides in him and he in God...". Christ is the Son, the anointed one, or the Messiah; any other doctrine contradicting this doctrine is not from God. The anointed one or the Messiah is mentioned 9 times in the old scriptures and the anointed One is clearly not God. It was Christ or the Messiah not God that came in the flesh that the bible states in 2 John 1:7 because He was indeed in heaven. God manifested in the flesh when God anointed Christ with the Holy Spirit and power and

Christ went out working miracles and healed the sick because God was with Him, the scriptures says in Acts 10:38. In other words, when God manifested Himself in Christ, the Holy Spirit entered Christ as seen in 1 Timothy 3:16: the behavior, deeds and intentions of Christ were that of God's. So, if one deals with Christ, then one can see the effect, and power of God. To put it on an earthly level, if a good metal is magnetized, the metal will exhibit the EXACT same essence of the permanent magnet. So, one cannot say show me the permanent magnet to see the power of magnetism. The good metal has shown it already, but yet it is not the permanent magnet.

Why do we believe that possessed people do exist (Christ exorcised many) and do not believe in the Holy Spirit entering the body?. Can we say that the possessed person is now the evil spirit? Once the evil spirit leaves, the person reverts to its original status. That is why God left Christ to die on the cross to show us that this is not a ploy; otherwise, if the power was left with Christ, He would have faked it and should not have felt pain or suffered. People surmised and use inferential reasoning on the gospel and rebelled against the explicit statements. People say Christ died and went to hades and then took the dead to heaven; yet, the gospel contradicts that fact in John 20:17 because Christ, Himself, has explicitly stated to Mary that He did not ascend to His God yet. Additionally, it is a blasphemy to say that the "living God" died. In the book of Daniel 6:26, it says that God is the living God steadfast forever and ever. Forever and ever has No disruptions (killing Him for 3 days breaks the scriptures). Didn't Christ ask, while on the cross, why His Father forsaken Him? Christ was able to forgive sins while teaching, why He did not forgive the soldiers while on the cross, but rather asked His Father to forgive them? Ans: The Holy Spirit left Him to truly die.

To reiterate, as stated in Mark 12:36, one can see the affirmation that the Lord (God) has said to my Lord (Christ) sit on my right hand, and I will make your enemy your footstool. So, if the man-made doctrine is indeed valid and Christ is no one other than God, then Christ was talking to Himself giving Himself moral support; this is definitely sacrilegious. Some churches began to manipulate the gospel to prove this earthly doctrine. I bring your attention to Revelation 1;8, where the Aramaic and the other 24 versions (NIV, New Living Translation, ESV, NASV, Christian Standard bible, ISV, Aramaic Bible etc.) of the gospels say "I am Alpha & Omega….says the Lord, "God"….' yet, in King James and two other versions, they omitted the word "God" to becloud the thinking of the followers. Worse yet, they added "Alpha & Omega" in Revelation 1:11 when Christ was talking whereas the others did not have that language. The warning in Revelation 22 was very clear to NOT add or delete anything to the book of the revelation; yet man's arrogance took over. At any rate, why man is using inferential reasoning to negate Christ's teachings? Since when Greek letters or alphabets were proofs for Christ and/or God?

If Christ is the same God of the old scriptures, He would have said that. He is not afraid of us and was not sent down to earth to play games and lie to us. Christ Himself repeated, throughout the entire New Testament, that He is the Messiah as written in John 4:26 or the Son as written in Mark 14:62. In Luke 22:48, Christ asked Judas if he is betraying the Son of Man with a kiss. He did not state that Judas was betraying God. Yet, in Mark 12:29, Christ, Himself said and flagged that the **first of all the commandments** is, "Hear O Israel the Lord Our God, is <u>One</u>…". Christ did not say, the Lord, Our God is formed in trinity.

Some extremist Jews swing to the other extreme and reject Christ as the Messiah by finding banal contradictions in the New Testament.

The same can be done for the old scriptures or the Tanakh such as (Genesis 32:30) when compared to (Exodus 33:20), and other places in the scriptures but that does not detract from its holiness and correctness. They try to attribute the verses in the Tanakh to David and other prophets. However, Isaiah 42 and 53 talked about the servant who brought light to the Gentiles. Neither David nor any of the old prophets brought any light to the gentiles. Additionally, the old scriptures gave the chronological arrival of the Messiah in Daniel 9 and the location of the birth of the Messiah in Micah 5.

PART TWO

THE SCRIPTURES THAT DISMANTLED THE DOCTRINE OF TRINITY

CHAPTER 3

THE SCRIPTURES THAT REFUTE TRINITY

The faithful should not just read this book and go back to his old erroneous way. The faithful, if truly faithful to God and His Christ, should open the scriptures and follow the evidence recited in this book. This is your only chance to redeem yourself, there will be no other time. On judgment day, you cannot blame your preacher, priest or any religious institution. You can only blame yourself as clearly explained by Abraham in Luke 16:23. In this instance, Abraham told the agonizing man in hades that his 5 brothers can avoid hades by reading and enforcing the scriptures. The Holy books should be the only source of divine conveyance. Unfortunately, man feels more comfortable with the teachings that are passed by man, whether they are supported by the Holy books or not. However, to be saved, one must follow the scriptures and not the rituals that are passed down from generation to generation. Christ drew a **clear distinction** between Himself and God in all His teachings in Judea and Aram. **Back in the Judeo-Christian era, the word "Lord" was used extensively to refer to God, the God of**

Israel, but also was used to refer to someone of higher stature. For example, in 1 Samuel 1:15, Hannah referred to her priest also as lord. The Father is called God, while people with God's authority on earth are called as gods. This could be discerned in 2 Corinthians 4:4, in Acts 12:22 and in the gospel of John 10:34 and 1 Corinthians 8:5. Additionally, Aramaic and Hebrew languages do not have both upper and lower cases; they have only upper case letters. So, in Hebrews and Aramaic language, all the words are written in capital letters. The current Greek language has upper and lower case letters. However, during the Roman empire era, the Greek language used only upper case letters mirroring the Aramaic and Hebrew languages. To this end, the word "GOD" represented both God and god. This style was used to write the New Testament. This type of manuscript writing is called "uncials". God is Lord but Lord is NOT necessarily God. The examples listed below are only a small fraction of what is written in the New Testament and the old scriptures about the nature of Christ. These examples are ironclad evidences that the trinity doctrine is faulty and is not substantiated in the Christian Holy books:

- Christ, in John 15:10, has instructed us to keep His commandments as He, Himself, has kept God's commandment. If the trinity doctrine is correct, then Christ has clearly misled us and made salvation harder to reach without a teacher. Yet, Christ has warned us about becoming teachers as stated in Matthew 23:8. How the doctrine of trinity dovetails with this affirmation by Christ? The doctrine of trinity has beclouded the scriptures and made the scriptures contradicting themselves.
- The mere fact that Christ worked miracles and raised the dead is not enough reason to label Him God. If raising the

dead is a criteria to classify an entity as God, then Peter, one of the disciples, should also be God. Peter raised Tabitha from the dead as explained in Acts 9:40.

- Right before His crucifixion as described in Luke 22:42, Christ has prayed and asked God if He can take the cup of suffering from Him. However, Christ qualified it by saying that it is **not His will but the Father's will** to decide. If the Son and Father are the same, then Christ was either hallucinating by talking to Himself and praying to Himself or bluntly deceiving us. If the trinity holds, then Christ's will must have been the Father's also. However, according to Christ's declaration, the wills are not the same. How the trinity solves this contradiction? Either way, the Council of Nicea has committed a blasphemy against God and His Christ.

- The New Testament is clear about the distinction between God and Christ. This distinction is evident in Acts 4:26, Revelation 20:6, Revelation 11:15, and Revelation 12:10. In Revelation 21:22 and Revelation 7:10, the New Testament talks about the Lord (God) and the lamb (Christ). In Revelation 3:12, Christ stated that the person who overcomes, He (Christ) will make him a pillar in the temple of His God. If trinity holds, then the New Testament should have said that the person will be a pillar in Christ's temple and not Christ's God temple. Trinity fails to be proven over and over. God is the Father of our Lord, Christ.

- When the high Jewish priest asked Christ as to His identity in Mark 14:61-62, Christ confirmed the priest's inquiry. The Priest asked Him if he was the Christ; the priest did not ask Him if He was God. Jesus acknowledged that He is the Christ. So, how the council of Nicea answers that exchange of information and affirmation? Did Christ mislead the followers and the high Jewish priest also?

- The New Testament stated, in the gospel of Luke 4;10, that the devil tempted Christ and asked Christ to jump from a high place. However, the devil did not tell Christ that His angels will rescue Him, but rather the devil said, that God will send His angels to prevent Christ's feet from hitting a stone. If Christ was that God, the devil would have known it, because devils recognize God and are fearful and scared of Him. The New Testament stated, in James 2:19, that the devils know that there is one God and they shudder.

- Christ, in Luke 4:18, has stated that the Spirit of the Lord is on Him because God has anointed Him to preach the gospel to the poor. How the trinity doctrine resolves this dichotomy? Was Christ not truthful with us and attempted to confuse His followers? The truth of the matter is that the trinity doctrine is an irreverence to God and Christ. This doctrine insulted all what is holy.

- In the first chapter of Mathew 1:1, it starts by stating the genealogy of Jesus Christ. It states that Christ is the son of David, son of Abraham. The Almighty Father, God, has no genealogy. It is a blasphemy to state that God has a genealogy or a starting point. Who is God? As the New Testament clearly states over and over; God is the Father of Christ, see 1 Peter 1:3, 2 Corinthians 1:3, and 2 John 1:3.

- The New Testament, in Hebrews 1:9, states that God has anointed Christ with the oil. Again, as one can discern, the Holy book is talking about God anointing Christ. The trinity doctrine is, once more, causing a dichotomy because if Christ is God, then God is anointing Himself. The assertion that God is anointing Himself does not pass any biblical interpretation or explanation.

- Christ, in the book of Revelation 3:12, has said that he who overcomes, Christ will make him a pillar in the temple of His God and Christ will write the name of His God. Why will Christ try to mislead us if He is indeed that God? Why Christ kept saying My God? Christ did not mislead us, it is man (bishops of the council of Nicea), to satisfy the Roman empire, confused and misled the followers and elicited the curse that Paul, the apostle, talked about in Galatians 1:8.

- In Hebrews 1:1-2, the New Testament states that in the old times, God spoke to us via the prophets, but in the last days, God spoke to us thru His Son.

- Christ Himself has said, in Mathew 24:36, that the last day or hour of the end of times no one knows, not even the angels in heavens, **nor the Son**, only the Father. That declaration unequivocally proves that the trinity doctrine is patently in error. If the Son and God are as "one" entity, then the Son would have known when the end of time will take place. **As was mentioned earlier, some churches attempted to hide that dichotomy by deleting the word "Son".**

- Throughout the New Testament, the statement that God raised Christ from the dead is rampant. Please read Ephesians 1:20, Romans 10:9, Acts 2:32, 1 Corinthians 15:15, Galatians1:1, Roman 8:11, 1 Corinthians 6:14. These repetitions, unmistakably, detract from the doctrine of trinity. The Holy book did not say Christ raised Himself as the current teachings proclaim. Additionally, the New Testament asserted over and over that Christ is the Servant of God as evidenced in Acts 3:13 and Acts 4:27.

- In the old scriptures, in Isiah 42:1, it says that **a servant of God**, His elect one,...and God will put His spirit upon Him and He will bring justices to the nations. None of the prophets mentioned in the old scriptures considered preaching to the gentiles. This is an evidence that the old scriptures have been fulfilled. The scriptures were referring to Christ. The One mentioned, in Isiah, is indeed the Son of God or Christ. God cannot put His own Spirit on Himself; this is biblically meaningless and does not pass any earthly or spiritual explanation.

- Christ reconfirmed, in Matthew 26:56, His position about the old scriptures by saying that all this was done so that the scriptures of the prophets might be fulfilled. This is another evidence that, to understand the nature of Christ, the old scriptures must be studied and tied to the New Testament. Also, in Matthew 26:24, Christ alluded again to the old scriptures by saying that the Son of man must go as it is written. Written where? The Christian gospels were not written when He was alive. The old scriptures were the only Holy books that were written at the time.

- The New Testament connects salvation to the admission of two separate declarations; one has to believe in Christ as our Lord and Savior and the second is to believe in our heart that God raised Him from the dead. This is evidenced in Romans 10:9 and 1 John 4:15.

- The high priest, in Mark 14:61 & 62, asked Jesus if He is the Messiah, the Son of the living God, to which Christ answered affirmatively. If Christ is God, then clearly Christ has misled us and did not tell the truth. Christ was not sent to earth to suffer and die to just mislead the followers.

- Christ, in Luke 4:18, while He opened the book of the prophet Isaiah, Christ read the statement that the Spirit of the Lord is upon Him because He has anointed Him to preach the gospel. This is another confirmation that the savior is exactly the entity that the old scriptures talked about. **Not once, in the old scriptures, it stated that God will become man and come to earth;** yet Christ stated that He came to fulfill the old scriptures. So, if the trinity is valid, then the old scriptures were wrong. No matter how one tackles this fake trinity doctrine, it spews nothing but irreverence to God and His Christ.

- Christ, in Luke 10:21, has made the following statement "...I thank you O father..." (New King James). Why will Christ try to confuse us and thank Himself if He is God?. Is the council of Nicea confirming that Christ has misled the followers throughout the whole New Testament? Was Christ sent to earth to preach vanity and show us how He can pat Himself on the back? Again, an ironclad evidence that the doctrine of trinity is faulty and man-made to satisfy the Roman empire.

- **Nowhere, in the New Testament, Christ has said to worship Him.** God is the same and does not change over time. God clearly stated in the Old Testament that He is a jealous God and that we must worship no one but Him. In the New Testament, on the contrary, Christ has instructed us to worship the Father (God). He further told us that everything we ask God in Christ's name, we should receive. Why Christ instructed us to do this if He is the same God that spoke to Moses in the old scriptures? The truthful answer is that Christ and God are **not** the same entities. The New Testament, in 1Timothy

2:5, clearly states that there is **one God** and **one mediator** between God and men, the man Jesus Christ. Christ is the mediator Who is interceding on our behalf to the Father as clearly stated in Roman 8:34.

- The New Testament, in the book of Revelation, Rev 1:18, states that Christ was dead and behold He is alive forevermore. **God, the Father, cannot and does not die**. If God died once, then He might die again. This is a pure blasphemy against God.

- The New Testament, in Hebrews 10:11-12, states that every priest stands daily offering sacrifices which can never take away sins, but this man after He had offered one sacrifice for sins forever, sat down at the right hand of God. A sacrifice must be offered to a higher authority and not to a lower one. The New Testament, in Hebrews 4:14-15, Hebrews 8:1, Hebrews 8:3 and Hebrews 10:21, states that Christ is our high priest over God's house. So, if Christ sacrificed His own spotless body for our sins, Whom did He sacrificed it to? If He is God, then did He sacrifice it to Himself? Is the Council saying that Christ is a masochist? Is the council saying that God offered His body as a sacrifice to a lower authority, man? A pure blasphemy against God and His Christ. The trinity doctrine engenders, nothing more than dichotomies and blasphemy.

- The New Testament, in Hebrews 9:14, states that Christ offered Himself without a spot to God. Here is the answer to the previous point. It is another indication that Christ is our high priest whose body was offered as a sacrifice to a higher authority, God, for our salvation. If the trinity doctrine is correct, then Christ offered Himself to Himself to please man, a doctrine that is sacrilegious, meaningless and has no biblical basis.

- The New Testament, in Hebrews 9:15, reiterates the fact that Christ is our mediator by stating that He is the Mediator of the new covenant. This reinforces what is written in 1Timothy 2:5 that there is one God, and one mediator between God and men, the man Jesus Christ. Christ is the mediator and He is interceding on our behalf to God as stated in Roman 8:34.

- The New Testament, in the book of Revelation, Rev. 1:1, states that the revelation of Jesus Christ, which God gave Him to show His servants. There is a doer here, God and someone being done on, Christ. This declaration states that God gave to Christ, it did not say God gave Himself.

- The New Testament, in Revelation 7:10, mentions that salvation comes from God who sits on the throne and from the Lamb. Since God decided to save us and send His only begotten Son to sacrifice Himself for the remission of our sins, then salvation comes from both the Father and the Son. If the Father is the same as the Son (if trinity holds), then the bible would have said salvation comes from God who is also the lamb. Again, you can see that the doctrine of trinity has no place in the bible. The proponents and defenders of this fake doctrine will get the "just" verdict on judgment day.

- The New Testament, in Hebrews 13:20, talks about the God of peace who brought up our Lord Jesus from the dead who is the shepherd of the sheep. That is an ironclad indication that the trinity doctrine is faulty at best. There is a doer who is God and someone being done on who is Christ. Christ or the Messiah was never portrayed as God in neither the old scriptures nor the New Testament.

- By His power, God raised our Lord Jesus Christ from the dead as it is clearly stated in 1Corinthians 6:14. The New Testament did not say that Christ has sort of fallen asleep and later risen from the dead as the churches state to implicitly and tacitly reinforce the idea of the trinity.

- Christ, in Mathew 24:5, has warned us about fake Christs who will come after Him stating that they are the Son of God. If Christ equates to God, then clearly Christ believes in multiple gods. As was discussed earlier, there is only one God and one begotten Son of God. Therefore, the doctrine of trinity is, again, not substantiated in the holy scriptures but rather detracts from the Holy book and contradicts it.

- The New Testament, in Hebrews 7:14, states that our Lord sprang out of Juda. If Christ is God, then we have said that God sprang out of Juda. In other words, God has a starting point and someone who made Him. This is a pure blasphemy against God. Christ, in Matthew 12:32, has warned us about blaspheming against the Holy Spirit or God.

- The most convincing two phrases in the New Testament that refute the doctrine of trinity are captured in the gospel of John 20:17 and Ephesians 1:3. After His resurrection, Christ told Mary not to cling to Him because He has not ascended to **His God and Her God**. Also, in Ephesians 1:3 where it said that God is the Father of our Lord Jesus Christ. If there is a God on top of a God, then we clearly have reverted to the idolatry era of the Roman empire.

- No priest, no pastor, no spiritual leader can save you; it is only Christ as He taught in the bible. As you recall, in Luke 16:23, when the rich man was sitting in hades looking up at Abraham, he told him to please dip his finger in water and cool his tongue for he was tormented. Then, he said to please go to his father's house and tell his 5 brothers so they do not wind up here. Abraham answered and told him that they have Moses (Torah) and the prophets (Nevi'im), they should hear these books. It is the teachings of the old and new scriptures that will save a person and not man.

- The New Testament, in Hebrews 1:4, states that **Christ was made** so much better than the angels. **God is not made**; the doctrine of trinity clearly induces a blasphemy against the Holy Spirit or God. The trinity is not substantiated anywhere in the old or the new scriptures.

- The New Testament, in Romans 10:9, states that to be saved one has to confess that Christ is Lord and that God raised Him from the dead. It did not say, if one believes that Christ raised Himself from the dead as the churches explicitly state. If one says that Christ is God and He died for 3 days, then the universe is left without a dominion for 3 days and that God might die again since He died once; a pure blasphemy against God!

- Just because the word became flesh, it does not mean the word is flesh. Notice that, in the Epistle of 1 John 5:7, it clearly states that the Father, Word, and Holy spirit are one in heaven; it did not say Christ. The word became flesh when God anointed Christ with the Holy Spirit and power as stated in Acts 10:38. Just like an evil spirit can enter a body, so can the Holy spirit. However, that does not mean that the Holy spirit is now flesh because, the spirit can leave the body again as Christ has attested to, while on the cross, in Matthew 27:46.

- The New Testament has stated, in Mark 6:4, that Christ has said that a prophet is not without honor but in His own country and among His own kin. Christ was referring to Himself in this statement. Why will Christ try to deceive us if He is God? Christ cannot be God because God is not a prophet.

- When the spirit is in the body, the behavior, words, deeds reflect the intent of the spirit, good or bad. The New Testament talked many times about Christ exorcising evil spirits from people as cited in Mark 1:25 and Mark 5:8-9. If one believes that evil spirit can enter the human body, then one should believe that a good spirit, and in particular the Holy Spirit, can also enter the body. One cannot have low unless there is high and one cannot define sweet unless there is bitter. Therefore, the Holy Spirit can indeed enter a body as stated, many times, in the New Testament. That is why Christ has said if you have seen Him, then you have seen the Father as stated in John 14:7. What it is meant by this declaration is that Christ words, deeds, behavior are all God's, but that does not mean that Christ is God. Otherwise, Christ has contravened the old scriptures which Christ, Himself, said He did not come to do as stated in Matthew 5:17. The old scriptures stated in Exodus 33:20 that no man can see God and live.

- Christ, in John 4:24, has stated that God is a spirit; yet, Christ had flesh and bones. Christ reiterated, in Luke 24:39, after His resurrection that flesh and bones is not a spirit. Who is the Council of Nicea to prove Christ wrong? Christ, Himself, has stated that God is a spirit. If one calls himself a Christian and does not follow Christ's teachings and words, then that person is pleasing man and not God. How can a person calls himself a Christian; yet, he ignores and casts aside what the savior has instructed us to do? Christ has instructed here to worship in spirit. God has sent His only begotten Son to save us. God spoke thru Christ to allow us to reach salvation. If we do not follow Christ's commandments, then we are just putting on a show and practicing rituals that are in vain. In 1 Samuel 15:19-22, Saul was anointed king over the 12 tribes of Israel; however, he did not fully obey God's instructions. Samuel, the prophet, told Saul that obeying the voice of God is better than sacrifices. Samuel, further stated, in 1 Samuel 15:22, that rebellion against God's words is as the sin of witchcraft. So, if one does not follow God's words, one risks being rejected by God Himself. God's words were spoken thru Christ; therefore, if one does not follow Christ's instructions and commandments, one risks being rejected by the Father.

- The New Testament, in Matthew 22:44, states that the Lord (God) has said to my Lord (Christ) that He will put all His enemies under His feet. How the Council of Nicea explains this mystery? Is the same God talking to Himself again? There is no sound explanation to the doctrine of trinity. This doctrine has elicited the curse that Paul, the apostle, has discussed in Galatians 1:8.

- Christ, in John 14:28, stated that the **Father was greater than Him**. Why will Christ try to deceive us if God and Him are the same entity as the trinity doctrine states? What is clearer than this statement? Christ did not come to suffer and die to just confuse and mislead us. Christ was in heaven prior to being sent to earth as clearly evident in John 6:38.

- Christ, in John 1:18, stated that **no man has ever seen God at any time**, only the Son. Is the council of Nicea contradicting Christ teachings by decreeing, with the trinity doctrine, that everyone, who was alive during Christ era, has seen God?

- The New Testament, in the first Epistle of Colossians 1:3, states that we should give thanks to God and the Father of our Lord Jesus Christ. Again, if the trinity was biblically based, it would have said that we give thanks to our Father who is our lord Jesus Christ. Clearly, it did not say that, but rather made the distinction between the two.

- The New Testament, in 2 Peter 1:13-21, addresses a blessing by stating that God should be blessed; God who is the Father of our Lord Jesus Christ. If Christ is God, then who is His Father? There cannot be a heavenly figure higher than God. If the trinity doctrine truly holds, then it should have read blessed is the Father who is our Lord Jesus Christ.

- The New Testament, in Acts 13:30, states that God raised Christ from the dead. There is a doer here who is God and someone being done on who is Christ. If Christ is God and He raised Himself, then He was not dead. The definition of dead quickly collapses. God wanted us to know that, if we follow His commandments, passed on to us by Christ and die just like Christ died, He will resurrect us again.

- Christ, in John 5:39, has instructed us to search the scriptures, for they testified of Him. Nowhere, in the old scriptures, it stated that Christ or the anointed one was God. Also, in Matthew 27:34-35, the New Testament reiterated what the old scriptures mentioned about parting His garments, casting lots so it can be fulfilled which was spoken by the prophet in the old testament in Psalm 22:18. Are we supposed to believe Christ or the council of Nicea? **If you believe in the trinity, then you have plainly ignored Christ teachings and the scriptures and followed a man's doctrine.** Christ talked many times in the bible about the blind leading the blind and that neither will enter the kingdom of heaven.

- The New Testament, in Romans 8:17, clearly draws a line of comprehension by stating that if we are children, then heirs, heirs of God and **joint heirs** with Christ. If one reflects on this statement alone, one realizes that the doctrine of trinity collapses rapidly with this declaration.

- The New Testament, in Romans 1:34, talks about Jesus Christ our Lord which was made of the seed of David according to the flesh and declared to be the son of God according to the spirit. If the trinity holds, then it should have replaced Son of God with God. Son of God and God are not the same; they are different entities. To put it on an earthly level, even though a son has the same DNA as the father, nonetheless the two have different fingerprints.

- The New Testament, in Romans 8:34, states that Christ is interceding on our behalf to God? Why it did not say, pray to Christ because He is God? God has clearly instructed us, in the old scriptures, to worship and pray to Him. If Christ is that same God, then He should not have changed His instructions and should have instructed us to worship Him. Yet, Christ told us explicitly to pray to the Father or God. Again, the trinity doctrine has no safe place in the old or new scriptures. This doctrine insults God and His Christ.

- God frowns on any doctrine that is introduced by man. The old scriptures stated, in Isaiah 29:13, that **one's worship is in vain if he follows man's rituals and teachings** instead of God's. The New Testament, in Romans 1:34, echoed the same declaration. The New Testament, in Mark 7:7, repeated the same language and reminded us of what the prophet

Isaiah has stated in the old scriptures. We must follow Christ's teachings and not man if we are after salvation. Paul warned us and Christ instructed us to pray to the Father. Christ said that God, the Father, is greater than Himself.

• Christ, in Mark 11:26, has clearly mentioned that if we do not forgive, the Father will not forgive our trespasses either. If the trinity doctrine is valid, then Christ clearly has misled His followers. If Christ was God, He would have used the pronoun "I" instead of the Father. Christ would have said "I" will not forgive you. To drive this idea even further, as you recall, while on the cross, Christ pleaded, in Luke 23:34, to the Father to forgive the people who crucified Him because they did not know what they have done. If He is God, Christ would have, again, used the pronoun "I". In other words, Christ would have said, I will forgive you. As one can surmise, either Christ misled us or the council of Nicea misled us. It is safer to go with the latter and affirm that the council of Nicea and its bishops committed this unspeakable act.

• How the trinity dovetails with what is written in Hebrews 3:1?, Jesus Christ is considered the Apostle and High Priest of our confession. God is neither a High Priest nor an Apostle. The trinity doctrine cannot dovetail with anything in the old scriptures or the New Testament.

• Christ, in John 7:28, stated that He did not come of Himself, but **He was sent by the Father whom we do not know**. If the Father and Son are the same, then we should have known the Father. However, Christ said you know me but you do not know the Father. Indeed, we have seen the behavior, deeds and characteristics of the Father (when God anointed Christ with the Holy spirit and power), but truly we have not seen

God because we cannot see God and live as explicitly stated in Exodus 33:20.

- Christ, in John 14:11, declared that He is in the Father and the Father is in Him. If the current churches use that declaration to justify the trinity; then one can use John 14:20 that states that Christ is in us and we are in Him to justify that we are also Christ and since Christ is God, then we are also God. A logic that is patently faulty.

- Christ, in John 14:10, stated that He **does not speak by Himself**, but the Father that dwells in Him, He does the work. This is another biblical proof that God indeed anointed Him with the Holy Spirit. As discussed earlier, when a spirit enters a body, the behavior of that entity mirrors that of the spirit, good or bad. In 2 Corinthians 5:19, the New Testament states that God was in Christ reinforcing the proclamation in Acts 10:38 that God has anointed Christ with the Holy Spirit.

- The old scriptures talked about Christ in Isiah 53 as a coming of a servant who will suffer. The old scriptures have been fulfilled as Christ has attested to. Christ came to earth, was ridiculed, suffered and died. God is not a servant and does not suffer.

- The New Testament, in 1 Timothy 3:16, clearly states that **God manifested in flesh, seen of angels**. God was manifested in flesh when the Spirit of God was put on Christ as declared in Acts 10:38. Again, unless you are a heavenly body, you cannot see God and live as stated in the old scriptures in exodus 33:20.

- The New Testament, in Hebrews 2:9, states that **Christ was made lower than the angels** for a little while to taste death. God can, at no time, be made lower than the angels; otherwise we have induced a blasphemy against God. Christ has warned us about blaspheming against God. **Christ, in Mark 3:29, has said that if we blaspheme against God or the Holy Spirit, we are in danger of eternal damnation.** After all, didn't God sent some angels to hell because they tried to be better than Him as clearly stated in 2 Peter 2:4. Trinity puts God under the angels reinforcing satan's cause.

- The New Testament, in 1Timothy 2:5, states that there is one God and one mediator between God and men that is the man Jesus Christ. Is the New Testament trying to deceive us? How the doctrine of trinity resolves this dichotomy? The Council of Nicea has confused, deceived and mutilated Christ teachings to satisfy the roman empire. The New Testament states, in Hebrews 8:6, that as Moses was divinely instructed, Christ got a better ministry by being the mediator between God and men. Who gave Him this ministry if not God? It is meaningless to say that Christ gave Himself something.

- Christ, in Matthew 12:32, has said if you say a word against Him, the Son, it will be forgiven, but not so against the Father or God. If the council decreed that Christ and God are the same, then Christ has clearly lied to us. Again, He did not come to earth to deceive us but to allow us to reach salvation. It is man who deceived us and not Christ.

- Christ, while on the cross, in Matthew 27:46, Christ shouted "...my God, my God why have you forsaken me?..." (New King James). If He is God, then who was Christ talking to? If Christ is God, is there another layer of gods above Him; maybe a God higher than a God. As you can quickly discern the odor of the multi gods religion of the Roman empire emanates from the trinity doctrine.

- Nothing is clearer that what is written in the bible of John 7:16 and John 12:49 where Christ has said that the doctrine He is passing to us is **NOT** His. Christ, further, stated that **He does not speak on His own authority**, but the **Father who sent Him gave Him command** what He should say. God does not take command from any one. If Christ is God, then Christ clearly lied and misled us.

- When one of disciples, in Mark 10:1, called Christ a good master, Christ replied and inquired as to why the disciple called Him good, Christ said that there is only one good, that is God. It does not mean Christ was not good, but **Christ was drawing a distinction between God and Himself**. Unfortunately, if a man is not destined to see with his eyes open or understand with his ears open, it shall not come to pass. The New Testament, in Matthew 13:14, reiterated the fulfillment of Isaiah, the prophet who stated that by hearing you shall hear and shall not understand and seeing, you shall see and not perceive.

- The New Testament, in James 1:13, states that **God does not get tempted by evil, yet Christ was tempted many times** by the devil as it is written in the gospel of Mark 1:13.

- The New Testament, in John 14:6, reiterates that no one will come to father except thru son. If Christ is God as the trinity states, why will Christ add this indirect complication to His teachings? He could simply state that He is God and we should follow the commandments, yet in John 7:16, Christ stated that the doctrine He is passing to us is NOT His. Christ instructions must be followed if we need to reach salvation. God has anointed Him with the Holy Spirit and power and put His Spirit on Him. If you do not follow the commandments and the teachings of Christ, then you can call yourself a Christian, but at **your own perils**.

- The New Testament, in John 5:19, states that the **Son can do nothing of Himself**. Again, what motive Christ had to deceive us or confuse us? Why will Christ make this declaration if He is the same God of Israel who was in the old scriptures? It is indeed man (council and its bishops) who convoluted and deceived the followers.

- The old scriptures, in Zechariah 9:9, stated that the king came lowly riding on a donkey. It came to fruition indeed that Christ fulfilled the old scriptures as He Himself declared; however, God does not ride donkeys because, as Christ has said, God is a spirit.

- The New Testament, in John 8:58, states before Abraham was "I Am", but that does not justify the doctrine that Christ is God. Are you saying that we cannot find any heavenly body or an angel who existed before Abraham? Christ was indeed in heaven and the **Father sanctified Him and sent Him** into the world as stated in John 10:36. Also, John the Baptist has stated in the New Testament, in John 1:30, that Christ is preferred before him because He was before him.

- Christ, in Matthew 22:31, reminded the people of what God has said in the old scriptures, saying have you not read which was spoken by God saying that He is the God of Abraham, the God of Isaac, the God of Jacobs. If the trinity is correct, then Christ would have clearly said "Me" instead of referencing "God". In other words, Christ would have said, have you not read which was spoken by "Me"; however, Christ did not even alluded to that at all because there is a difference between God and Christ.

- The New Testament talked about Christ as a prophet in Luke 24:19. It said that concerning Jesus of Nazareth who was a prophet mighty in deed and word before God and all the people. The bible did not say Christ was God. God is neither a prophet nor an angel.

- The New Testament, in Ephesians 1:3, states that God is the father of our Lord Jesus Christ. If Christ is God then who is His father? Is there somebody higher than God? Many dichotomies resulted from the error promulgated by the Council of Nicea. When Christ was being baptized in the river of Jordan, it said heaven opened up and a voice from heaven stated that Christ was God's is His beloved son with Whom He is well pleased. How the Council explains this one? Was Christ lauding himself? Whose words were those that came from heaven?

- Christ, in John 14:28, has said that the **Father is greater than Him**. If Christ is God, then Christ bluntly deceived us. The trinity doctrine has created a religion that is not substantiated by either the old scriptures or the New Testament. Again, He did not come to earth to suffer and die to just deceive us.

- In 2 John 1:9, the New Testament states that if we follow Christ teachings, we will have BOTH the Father and the Son. The term "BOTH" indicates they are two distinct entities and not one as the trinity declares.

- Christ, in Matthew 5:17, has said that He did not come to abolish the old scriptures, but to fulfill it. The old scriptures talked about the coming of the Messiah to which Christ attested to in John 4:25, 26. **Nowhere, in the old scriptures, it said that the anointed one or the Messiah was God**. Then, how can man make this connection? Again, this error of trinity was endorsed by the Roman empire and supported by these betrayers whom the churches call saints. The New Testament, in Luke 23:56, showed us that the followers and the disciple of Christ followed the commandments by observing the Sabbath. At times, we see that Christ did not observe the Sabbath, not because He abolished it, but because being filled with the Holy Spirit, His actions were God's. The commandments are set for men to follow and not for the Son of God.

- The disciples, in Acts 2:22, addressed the people by saying men of Israel, hear these words Jesus of Nazareth, a **man approved of God**. The disciples did not say Jesus of Nazareth is God. **Approved of God is not the same as God.**

- The New Testament, in Acts 3:15, states that we killed the Prince of life whom God raised from the dead, where we are witnesses. The disciples did not say that Christ raised Himself. The notion that Christ raised Himself will quickly run aground because it means that Christ has not really died. Again, the Council of Nicea has insulted God and His Christ.

- The New Testament, in James 4:12, states that God alone, who gave the law, is the judge. God of Israel, as spoken of in the old scriptures, is the entity who gave the law to Moses. Additionally, the New Testament, in Matthew 25:31-46, states that Christ will come in His glory and all the angels with Him and He will sit on His glorious throne. The king will say to the people on the right "come you who are blessed by my Father". Again, as you can see from that declaration that, even on judgment day, Christ was sent to collect the good and chosen one that God has already judged. **Christ did not say that He will judge the people.** Christ and the angels will come to collect the weeds to be put in bundles to be burnt and the wheat will be taken to the barn as stated in Matthew 13:30. God will judge the world's thru His Son, the man whom He ordained as clearly stated in Acts 17:31. Only God will judge; God judges the heart as stated in the old scriptures in 1 Samuel 16:7 and Jeremiah 17:10.

- The New Testament, in Acts 5:30, states that **God of our fathers raised up Christ** whom you killed and hanged on a tree. God of our fathers is a term used throughout the old scriptures. God is the same in the past, the present and the future.

- The New Testament, in the first Epistle of Colossians 1:15, states that Christ is the image of the **invisible God**. Again, invisible means that no one can see. No one can see God and live as explicitly stated in the old scriptures in Exodus 33:20. Christ behavior and deeds reflected that of the Father when God anointed Christ with the Holy Spirit and power. Therefore, Christ is the image of God, but that does not mean He is God. Let's put this idea on an earthly level or as Christ did with parables by comparing what is heavenly to what is earthly. If you make a copy of an original document, notwithstanding that the copy mirrors the full content of the original document, can you declare that the copy is the original or the innate document?. If this document is your passport, can you travel or move to another foreign country using a copy of the passport? How then you are seeking to go to eternal life presenting a copy or an image of God? Christ clearly instructed us to worship the Father or God. Additionally, in 1 John 4:12, the New Testament states that no one has seen God at any time. 1 kilo of iron is EQUAL to 1 kilo of cotton; but certainly iron is NOT cotton.

- Jesus asked Peter, in Mathew 16:15-17, to tell Him who Peter thinks Christ was. Peter replied and said that He was Christ, the Messiah, the son of the living God. After that answer, Christ replied and blessed Simeon Bar-Jonah (Peter). How the council of Nicea answers that one? Were Christ and Peter in on the same game to mislead us?

- **The old scriptures, in 1 Samuel 15:29, stated that God is not a man and as such He should not relent or change His mind.** The New Testament talked about Christ as being the Son of God but also refer to Him as the Son of man. The disciples, in Acts 2:22, addressed the people by saying men of Israel, hear these words Jesus of Nazareth, a **man approved of God.** So, how the council of Nicea addresses this dichotomy? The trinity clearly contradicts what is written in the old scriptures and contradicts Christ's teachings in the New Testament. Christ has said that He did not come to abolish the old scriptures. If one uses the trinity as a factual doctrine, then one has made Christ into a liar. The trinity doctrine is an insult to God and Christ.

- The New Testament was written in the first century to capture the teachings of the apostles and the teaching of Christ's instructions. **The trinity doctrine did not come into play and put on solid ground until around the fourth century. Nowhere in the New Testament does the word trinity appear or being mentioned.** Not once Christ discussed this doctrine; au contraire, Christ kept it on a monotheistic level by kept repeating the Father or God. The aforementioned fact is an ironclad evidence that the trinity was not preached or considered during the first century and prior when the teachings of the apostles were still fresh. **This addition is definitely a sacrilegious addition to what Christ and the apostles imparted.** This addition is deserving of the curse that Paul, the apostle, mentioned in Galatians 1:8. Look around you and see what is happening in the world.

- Christ, in John 10:30, stated that the Father and Him are one. That does not mean that He is the Father; if Christ was the Father, God, He would have said that He is the Father. If one looks at John 17:20-22, one can discern that Christ was praying to the Father to render His followers to become one with each other and also to become one with Him and the Father. Using the faulty Trinitarian logic, one can say that the followers are also God; a pure folly. Also, in Ephesians 5:31, Christ stated that man will leave his parents and is joined to his wife and the two shall become ONE flesh. Using the faulty logic of the Trinitarian doctrine, one can assume that the man and his wife are also ONE person.

- Trinitarians believe that God came down on His own and became a man. This notion is clearly debunked by Christ declarations in several places in the New Testament. Christ clearly stated that He did not come down on His own, but His Father (God) sent Him down. Christ stated that He did not speak on His own authority (does God need someone to give Him authority to speak?), Christ stated that the words He spoke were Not His, but the Father's. Additionally Christ stated that He cannot do anything by Himself. All of these declarations can be discerned in the gospel of John specifically in (John 12:49), (John 5:30), (John 8:42), (John 14:10), (John 6:38), (John 7:16), (John 14:23-24), (John 8:28), (John 5:19) and other places in the bible. The council of Nicea introduced a fabricated Christ and Paul the apostle predicted that people from within will distort the teachings and preach a different Jesus (2 Corinthians 11:4).

The below are only few affirmations from the gospel distinguishing between the Father or God and the Son:

- In 2 John 1: 9, it states "… whoever does not abide in the doctrine passed by Christ <u>does not know God</u> and the one who does abide in it has <u>BOTH</u>, the Father and the Son. <u>"Both" means more than one</u>.
- 1 Corinthians 8: 1-13, "There is one God, the Father of Jesus.."
- 1 Peter 1:3 "…blessed be God the Father of our Lord…";
- 2 Corinthians 11:31 '..God and father of Christ.."; ;
- 2 John 1:3 "..Grace from God the Father and from the Lord Jesus Christ, the Son of the Father";
- 1 Timothy 2:5 "..There is one God and one mediator between God & man, the Man Jesus Christ.."; This is a simple that a child can understand.
- 1 John 2: 22 "…a liar who denies that Jesus is Christ, but is the antichrist who denies the Father **and** the Son…";
- 1 Corinthians 8:6 "..There is One God of Whom are all things and One Lord through whom are all things…" – Christ implements the Father's will.
- Ephesians 1:3 "..The God and Father of Christ…". How many Gods on top of God we should have if we are a monotheistic religion?
- Mark 13:32 "that day & hour no one knows, not the angels, <u>nor the Son</u>, only the Father..". Isn't God all knowing? If the

Son is God, then either Christ lied or man lied; it is safer to go with the latter.

- In Luke 4:18, it states that the Spirit of the Lord is upon Me and today the scriptures have been fulfilled. Did God put His own Spirit on Himself?

- John 6:27 "...God, the Father has set the seal on Christ...". There is a doer and someone being done on, unless Christ came down to deceive us as the trinity, a man made doctrine, infers. He did not come down from heaven to die for our sins, so we can turn around and create a doctrine that contradicts and insults Christ and think we are getting salvation. Christ knew that this will happen and warned us as to what will happen in Matthew 7: 21-22.

The Christian historians wrote that the roman empire tried from the beginning to pervert the gospel of Christ and finally succeeded with Constantine I. At the end, and history testifies that Rome finally managed to infuse paganism into Christianity and called the ones who refused to go along, "heretics" and persecuted them just like they did the Jews. With the emergence and enforcement of the trinity doctrine in the 4th and 5th century, more Christians were killed on the hands of Christians than any other times wrote the historians. One historian, Will Durant, explained this persecution and killings of Christians by Christians. Satan drove the wedge between Christians!

Man created an earthly doctrine and followers were asked to have faith in that doctrine. <u>Having faith in God's doctrine is one thing and having faith in a man's doctrine is another</u>. The New Testament is riddled with explicit affirmations that God raised Christ from the dead such as in (1 Corinthians 6:14, (Roman 8:11, Ephesians 1:20, Acts 2:32, Colossians 2:12, Acts 10:40). One statement really stands out, in <u>Romans 10: 9,</u> where our **salvation** even hinges on <u>**two conditions**</u>; the faith in Christ and the belief in our heart that God has indeed raised Christ from the dead, not Christ got up on His own after three days as they proclaim. In Colossians 2:8, it warns us about the deceivers who use tradition to distort the gospel and preach a different Jesus.

If we teach a doctrine that is not in the bible and worse yet, we ignore the bible's affirmations, then we are rebelling against God because God spoke to us thru Christ. In Hebrews 1:1-2, the gospel stated that in the old days God spoke to us thru the prophets, but in the last days God spoke to us thru His Son. Certainly, the prophets were not God. Rebellion against God's instructions is a sin as written in 1 Samuel 15:23.

People are grasping at any banal statement to justify this man made doctrine called the trinity even to the point of rejecting God's words. <u>They have replaced God's instructions with the teaching of the elders and traditions.</u> Christ rebuked the Pharisees, Sadducees, scribes not because they were Jews and followed the scriptures. Rather, He rebuked them because they did exactly what is being done today, ignored God's instructions in the scriptures and replaced them with traditions and teaching of the elders as can be gleaned from Matthew 15: 3,6.

CHAPTER 4

DISMANTLING THE PILLARS OF TRINITY

Despite the preponderance of the evidence that stack against the trinity doctrine, the Christian spiritual leaders rely on inferential declarations in the scriptures to prove the trinity. The followers accept, by faith, these declarations without uncovering the essence of these declarations. I do not blame the followers, I blame the teachers because, in doing so, they have violated Christ warnings by refraining from teachings as discussed earlier in Matthew 23:8. The erroneous teachings of this fake doctrine is going to elicit a stricter judgment on judgment day as discussed in James 3:1. In dismantling the pillars of trinity, I will attempt to stay in unison with Christ's methods. Christ spoke in parables using earthly level explanations to allow us to better grasp the scriptures. To this end, my explanation will be based on an earthly explanation and a spiritual explanation (based on the scriptures). I will start with the alpha and the omega declaration

- The New Testament, in the book of Revelation, Rev. 1:1, states that the revelation of Jesus Christ, which God gave Him to show His servants. There is a doer here (God) and someone being done on (Christ); God gave to Christ, it did not say God gave Himself.

In the same chapter of Revelation, Rev 1:8, the New Testament states that Christ is the alpha and the Omega, the beginning and the end. Using the trinity as a basis, the churches construed this to mean that Christ is God. Below is the counter-argument to this hollow justification:

o **The writer of this first chapter could not have in one sentence stated that God, the Father gave Christ, to continue few words later and contradict himself by saying Christ is God and He gave Himself. Christ is the first Son of God and the last son of God.** The first and the last mean that Christ is the first begotten Son of God and the last One. No begotten Son of God came before Him and no one will come after Him until His second coming as was explained in the same paragraph of Rev 1:8 that the Lord who is and who was and who is to come.

The translation from the original writing to English has induced this confusion. In the Aramaic bible, it says Christ is the original and the fulfillment, which is what Christ confirmed by saying that He was sent down to fulfill the old scriptures.

The second point that they use to show the followers that the trinity is a valid doctrine is that the Word became flesh.

• In the New Testament, in John 1:1-2, states that in the beginning was the word, and the Word was with God and the Word was God. Also, in John 1:13, the gospel states that the Word became flesh and dwelt among us. Just because the Word became flesh does not mean the Word is flesh. The Word became flesh when God anointed Christ with the Holy Spirit and power as stated in Acts 10:38 when God spoke thru Christ (God words were spoken thru Christ). The verb "become" is not synonymous with the verb "is"; one has to look at the original or the innate status and not the transitional state. To put this on an earthly level, water, under certain conditions, can "become" a gas (vapor), but that does not mean that water "is" a gas. To put it under another earthly level, when a good metal is magnetized, it will exhibit the same exact behavior as the permanent magnet, but that does not mean that this good metal is now a permanent magnet. Magnetism can be removed from the good metal and reverts back to its original or innate state. This is exactly what happened with Christ when He was on the cross; Christ words corroborate this explanation. Christ, in Matthew 27:46, cried out to God by inquiring as to why God has left, forsaken or reverted Him to His original status? Below is the counter-argument to this hollow explanation:

o   The foregoing explanation will break the back of the trinity doctrine. As you recall in the old scriptures in Exodus 3:1-5, God spoke to Moses thru a burning bush. So, in reality, God or the "Word" became a burning bush. That bush spoke God's Words to Moses; notwithstanding that the bush did not dwell or walk among us but rather was inanimate object, should we consider the burning bush as God and start worshipping it? This is exactly what happened when God spoke thru Christ. Christ instructed us in John 4:24 to worship God who is the Holy Spirit.

As you can see that the reasoning used by the churches to prop up this fabricated and lifeless doctrine of trinity is not valid. This doctrine is created by man to please the Roman empire and it is not substantiated anywhere in the bible.

The third argument they use to justify the trinity is the phrase from the old testament about God creating man in His own image

- The churches like to argue that the old testament stated that God has created us in His image as recited in Genesis 1:27; therefore, Christ is God because His image is identical to ours. Below is the counter-argument to this hollow explanation:
  o Don't you remember what the gospel of John 10:35-36 stated? The scriptures labeled us also gods. Father sanctified Christ and sent Him to die. The old scriptures and the New Testament, in Matthew 19:4, indeed said that God created us in His image, male and female, but it does not mean God has a female and male organs. What a blasphemy! What God stated is that, as He has dominion over us, we (as gods) have dominion over all things on earth from animals, to birds, to fish etc.. God has said that we are all gods, but it does not mean that we are the same as our Father in heavens. Also, in Psalm 82:6, it talks about men as being gods.

The fourth argument the churches invoke to validate this fake trinity doctrine is to use what God, the Father, has said to His only begotten Son, Christ

- The churches like to argue that, in Hebrews 1:8, God has said to His Son "Your throne O God is forever and ever" (New King James); therefore, Christ is God. Are the churches saying that we are reverting to the old days of the Roman empire of having a god on top of a god? If the churches truly believe in monotheism, then they should have known that Christ cannot be the same Almighty God, the Father; otherwise, they have contravened monotheism. Below is the answer to this hollow argument:

  o The blindness and the dullness of their understanding have truly consumed their knowledge and wisdom. As this book explained earlier, that there is only one God; others are called gods so the scriptures can be fulfilled. The Father is called God, while people with God's authority on earth are called gods. This could be discerned in 2 Corinthians 4:4, in Acts 12:22 and in the gospel of John 10:34. In Hebrews and Aramaic language, all the words are written in capital letters. During the Roman empire era, the Greek language that was invoked to write the New testament utilized only upper case letters mirroring the Aramaic and Hebrews languages. This type of manuscript writing is called "uncial". The New Testament clearly stated that God, the Father, has spoken in that fashion to His Son. So, there is a divine entity speaking to His Son. It is a blasphemy to interpret this declaration by saying that God was talking to Himself. This book also talked about Christ being a king and being anointed with the Holy Spirit and power as reflected in Acts 10:38. The anointment is eserved for kings who sit on thrones. Saul, as this book discussed earlier, was also anointed as a king over the 12 tribes of Israel, but his throne was not maintained forever because he did not fully obeyed God's commandments. In John 15:10, Christ told us that He kept God's commandments; this is why His throne will be maintained forever. Being anointed as a king, who sits on the throne and being labeled god, does not mean that this figure is the almighty Father, God.

Here are few lifeless justifications that some people use to prop up the man-made doctrine:

- In John 1, it says that the Word became flesh. To justify this lifeless doctrine, they surmised that Christ is God. Using the same logic, in Exodus 3: 4, God spoke to Moses thru a burning bush and so the Word became a burning bush; the bush is not God. Is it?
- In John 14:11, Christ stated that He is in the Father and the Father is in Him (conclusion: man's doctrine is correct). But wait, continue reading…in John 14:20, Christ stated That He is in the father, we are in Him and He in us. Are we supposed to interpret this as "us" also being Jesus and God?
- In John 10:30, Christ said that Him and the Father are one (conclusion: man's doctrine is correct), but wait let's look at John 17:21, Christ prayed to the Father that all the disciples be <u>one</u> in them and <u>one</u> in the Father and Christ. Are all the disciples also the Father and Christ?
- In Matthew 19:5, Christ talked about a man leaving his parents and joining his wife and the two will become <u>one</u> flesh. Are we saying here also that the wife and the husband are the same person? All of these are inferential reasoning.

- In Roman 8:16-17, the scriptures says that if we are sons of God and as such heirs, then also joint heirs with Christ. If Christ is God, the Father, then Christ is inheriting Himself. How far are we willing to negate and detract from the scriptures to solidify this man-made doctrine?

- In John 14:9, Christ said when one sees Him, one will see the Father (conclusion: Man's doctrine is correct). Yet, Christ explains His statement by declaring that <u>He does not speak on His own authority</u>, but the Father who dwells in Him. If Christ is God, then He deceived us once more because it is indeed His authority. So, was Christ not truthful with us? God forbid!

- In John 14:28, Christ said that the Father is greater than Him. How the trinity undo this dichotomy?

- In Genesis 1:26, it states that God said, let <u>Us</u> create man in <u>Our</u> image. God was talking to Christ because Christ was in heaven (John 6:38). Yet, man proclaims that since Jesus has a humanly body, then He is that God. Well what happened about God's image who is a spirit (John 4:24), didn't God said <u>OUR</u> image? God told us that He created the worlds thru His Son (Hebrews 1:1-2) corroborating Genesis 1:26. Image is not the humanly shape, because God is a spirit, but rather the image is the dominion. As God and Christ have dominion over us, we are made to have dominion over the fish, birds, animals....

- In John 20: 28, Thomas exclaimed after he was admonished by Christ ("...do not be unbelieving, but rather believing.."), "My Lord and My God' replied Thomas (conclusion; man's doctrine is correct). How many times, a person talking to another realized that he has erred and pronounced "my

God, sorry"?. Not because the person we are speaking to is God. Not once Thomas called Christ God before His death. Not any of the disciples called Christ God <u>at any time</u>, but rather called Him the Messiah or the Son (Matthew 16:16). Let us, for one moment, assume that Thomas meant that exclamation, how gratifying to Christ to know that we have taken Thomas exclamation to justify a "deceptive" truth over His own affirmation which is "all" the truth stating, in John 20:17, that He did not ascend to Mary's God and <u>His God</u>? Should the reaction of people take precedence over what's Christ taught us? In Acts 10:25, Cornelius knelt and worshipped Peter. Should we consider Cornelius's action as a sign to worship Peter instead of God?; certainly Peter was not God even though he raised the dead.

- In Revelation 22:8-12, it refers to the entity Who spoke to john as an angel, yet this entity instructed John to not worship Him, but He told him to worship God. That entity is no other than Christ because He continued and stated that He is coming soon in Revelation 22:12. Also, He told John that He is one of the brethren the prophets. If He is indeed an angel and never came down to earth, how then can He be one of the brethren the prophets. Only Jesus, as a heavenly figure, Who came in the flesh (1 John 4:2). The sons of God are indeed the heavenly figures such as the angels as depicted in Job 1:6

If this man-made doctrine is valid, then Christ was not truthful with us throughout the entire New Testament and the gospel was all in error. One example stands out as can be discerned in Matthew 12:32 and Luke 12:10. If a man says a word against Christ, then according to this man-made doctrine, he is doomed because Christ is God; yet, <u>Christ said just the opposite</u>. Also, in 1 Corinthians 11:3, it states that the head of every man is Christ and the head of woman is man and the head of Christ is God. If Christ is God, as this man-made doctrine proclaims, then the woman is man and the man is Christ. A dichotomy that cannot be resolved.

In conclusion, the trinity is the basic divine elements of the idol worshippers. In ancient Egypt, there was a hymn to the god amun stating that <u>one cannot have a god</u> unless it is formed in trinity. Trinity is nowhere to be found in the New Testament or the old scriptures; however, the old testament talked about God's hate of this type of abomination. The Babylonians had baal (father), Ishtar and tammuz(son). Baal is mentioned many times in the old scriptures and in Ezekiel 8: 14, God expressed His disdain of that type of worship of tammuz, where the women were crying for tammuz, the son god. Did Christ come to start a new religion or came to fulfill the old scriptures? If one follows Christ, then he will pick the latter as explained in Matthew 5:17. Is this type of Trinitarian god forming mentioned in the old scriptures? The good Jews never believed in the trinity (remember that Christ's disciples and apostles were Jews). Some religious institutions tell their followers that the Christian trinity is different than the pagan trinity because the trinity of the pagans had a female in it. That is a deception also; in ancient Egypt, the trinity of amun, re, ptah were all males. Not once Christ or the apostles talked about the trinity. This concept surfaced and was put on a solid footing in the 4th and 5th century with the help of Rome, the pagan nation who disassociated Christ teaching from Judaism and started a totally new religion mingled with paganism. In all His teachings, Christ told us that He did not come to abolish the law or the scriptures, but to fulfill them as cited in Matthew 5:17-18 and Matthew 26:54; how then we started a new religion and created new doctrines?. As a matter of fact,

Christ and the apostles taught on the Sabbath and observed it as can be seen in Luke 4:16, Acts 17:2, Luke 23:56, Acts 13:14, Acts 16:13, and Acts 17:2. Christ, in all His teachings, did not transgress the Sabbath. He broke the Pharisaic rules and traditions because they decided on what is holy and what is not. The commandment stated to keep the Sabbath holy and Christ showed the hypocrites that to help and love others is holy. In Matthew 5:18 and Matthew 15:17-18, Christ said that till heaven and earth pass, not one jot or title from the law shall pass until it is all fulfilled. In Luke 16:17, Christ reiterated again that it is easier for heaven and earth to pass than one title of the law to fail. His disciples who were Jewish still observed the law; as a matter of fact, Paul, the main apostle for the gentiles, in Romans 3:31, stated "...do we then make void the law through faith, Certainly not! On the contrary we establish the law...". Rome has perverted the gospel of Christ and managed to change the Sabbath to Sunday because the pagan nation worshipped the sun god on Sunday.

Socrates of Constantinople, a reliable Christian historian, recorded in his book that "...the Christians of Alexandria and of Rome began to preach a different gospel by failing to observe the Sabbath whereas the other early churches continued with the original teachings..." (history book 5, Chapter 22). At the end, thru sheer size and numbers, the two churches of Alexandria and Rome prevailed.

People who are following a doctrine that is not in the bible are taking a different path at their own perils. Too many souls are riding on this man-made doctrine. Man is fallible and was born in sin. No pastor, no priest, no bishop no pope can save a soul. These people are striving to save their own souls let alone others. It is the gospel that grants the salvation because it says that **Christ trampled death thru the gospel as cited in 2 Timothy 1:10).** In Luke 16:29, Christ talked about the conversation between the rich man in hades and Abraham.

Abraham told the rich man that his 5 brothers can be saved if they heed the scriptures. Abraham did not tell the tormented man that his brothers need to see the rabbi or follow the traditions of the elders. It is God's word and obedience that pave the way to salvation. If a man is stuck in the knowledge that is passed down from generation to generation and <u>ignored what is written</u> in the bible, he will not be convinced of the "truth" even if he sees a dead man rises from the dead as stated in Luke 16: 31.

In Matthew 28:19, it states to go and baptize in the name of the Father, Son and Holy Spirit. Baptism is an affirmation for repentance as explained in Mark 1: 4. When one repents, one returns to God. God is a <u>Holy Spirit</u> as stated in John 4:24. God was clearly identified in the New Testament as the <u>Father</u> over and over. No one has seen God at any time and only His <u>Word</u> was passed to us thru the prophets and finally thru the Christ as stated in Hebrews 1:1-2. So, when we baptize we are going back to God who is the <u>Father, Word and Holy Spirit</u> as confirmed by 1 John 5: 7. To make sure that we do not forget that Christ's blood allowed that return to God and that God's Word was spoken last thru the Son, the Word was replaced with the Son. If a man's name is Joe Tell, calling him Mr Tell, Mr Joe Tell or Mr Joe makes him three entities in one or they are the same person under different names?

In Philippians 2:6, it states that Christ being in the form of God... <u>Being in the form of God is not the same as being God</u>, because in later verses in Philippians 2:9, it says that God exalted Him and gave Him a name above all others. Exalting oneself is a vanity and not godly. In John 6:27. It says that God put His seal on Christ. If Christ is made in the form of God, who made Him like a God? In Exodus 7:1, God told Moses that He made him also as a god to the Egyptians. Certainly, Moses is not God.

Nothing is clearer than the book of Revelation on the distinction between God and Christ:

- Revelation 7:10 "…Salvation comes from God and the lamb…". Salvation came from <u>Both</u> God and Christ; God who sent Christ down (John 6:38) and from Christ, the Lamb (John 1;29) who died for us. Christ offered His body as a sacrifice for atonement to God (Ephesians 5:2, Hebrews 10:12); one cannot offer a sacrifice to oneself, that is absolutely sacrilegious.

- Revelation 21:22 "..God and the Lamb are (<u>not is</u>) the temple in the new Jerusalem.

- Revelation 3:21 "Just as Christ sat with His Father on the throne, the "saved" will sit with Christ on His throne ..".but certainly the "saved" is not Christ! . A throne does not equate with God, for 24 elders will also be on their thrones as cited in Revelation 4:4

- Revelation 3: 5 "..Whoever overcomes, I will confess his name before My Father…"

- Revelation 3:12 "Whoever overcomes, I will make him a pillar in the temple of My God…"

- Revelation 12:10 "…the kingdom of our God and the power of <u>His</u> Christ…"

- In John 1:36 it clearly tells us that Christ is the lamb of God.

- People are so confused by the doctrine of trinity that they zoom in on one verse and throw the rest of the statement in the same chapter. For example, in Hebrews 1:8, they stated that God said to Christ "your throne O God is forever,…" therefore, trinity is valid. Let us just examine this alone, if we are a monotheistic religion, the trinity poses a problem already; how can God said to Christ O God violating the first commandment? That makes us having 2 Gods...violating the monotheistic theory in the first place. If one continue reading Hebrews, one can see that in Hebrews 1:9, it clarified this quickly by saying "That Christ's God has anointed Christ with the oil of gladness more than His companions. Psalms was in the old testament and that did not confuse the Jews who all along knew that there is one God. Christ's disciples were also Jews; they were not confused. Even Christ has talked about gods in John 10:36 and said "...isn't it written in the old scriptures and the scriptures **cannot be broken** that you all are gods, then why are you saying that I am blaspheming, since the Father has sent me, because I am calling myself the Son of God...?". The original writing of Hebrews, Aramaic and old Greek did not have upper and lower alphabet; all were upper case letters.

- The shield of trinity symbol or the "Scutum Fidei" shown below mirrors the trinity of the idol worshippers. In the pagan world, they had the arrangement of 3 distinct persons and each one is a god. To attract pagan to Christianity, the betrayers of Christ distorted the teachings of Christ and the apostles and merged the 3 gods into one giving the fake appearance of monotheism. Yet, Christ in (John 17:1-3), clearly stated that the Father is the ONLY true God unequivocally debunking the trinity doctrine. God is one, not as the doctrine of trinity declares which is 3 distinct entity, but yet they are the same God. To debunk the idea of the trinity even further, the New Testament is the fulfillment of the old scriptures as Christ attested to in (Matthew 5: 17). The old scriptures in (Proverbs 8:22-30) stated that God brought forth Christ and this is repeated again by Christ in (John 16:24) and (John 17:5).

The bible is clear to state that Christ is the "begotten" Son of God in (John 3:16), not God. Begotten means brought into existence and in this case, God cannot be begotten, but Christ was begotten by God (Proverbs 8:22-30) before the creation of the world. Additionally, in (1 Corinthians 15:24-28), it clearly states that at the end of times, Christ will hand over the kingdom to God the Father and the Son will also be made subject to God, so God will be all in all. Additionally, why will Christ lie and state 4 times in one verse in (Revelation 3:11-12) that the Father is His God? The trinity doctrine truly blasphemes against everything holy and detracts from the suffering of Christ.

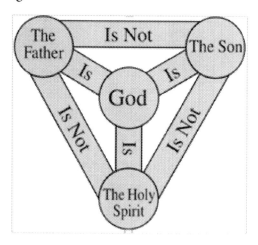

Man's doctrine and creeds are just that...earthly!!. People are negating the old and new scriptures to stand by this man's doctrine and creeds. Clearly in Numbers 23:19, it says that God is not a man or a son of man. Are we willing to render the old scriptures invalid because of this man-made doctrine? Christ said that He did not come to change any of the old scriptures, but rather to fulfill them. Also,

Christ said that the scriptures cannot be broken as written in John 10:35. The old scriptures are upright and true.

I pray that the Spirit will make the reader knowledgeable of His power this day and everyday in His Spirit (if it is in His will), so he can serve God and His Christ (Acts 4:26-27) because thru the authority of the Father, Christ who is God's begotten Son (Acts 3:13-15, Acts 4:30) created the worlds (Genesis 1:26, Hebrews 1:1-2). As Genesis 1;26 has stated that God was talking to someone in heaven about creating man in Their image and creating the worlds which Hebrews 1:1-2 reiterated that God created the worlds thru His Son, Christ. Therefore, is it wrong then to say that God created the worlds? To put it on an earthly level, if a construction company "A" sent a roofer to build the roof on house, is it wrong to say that company "A" built the home/roof? Christ will come back again with the heavenly figures to judge the worlds because God has stated that He will judge the worlds thru His Son as called in Acts 17:31. Christ will judge us according to our deeds and our obedience to the Father as stated in Matthew 25:34-36.

Note that, even on judgment day, Christ will state "...come you blessed of My Father !!!!..." –Matthew 25: 34

Truly the God of Jesus (John 20:17) is the Father of glory (Ephesians 1:17)

EPILOGUE

I close by saying that the trinity is an impediment to Christ. Christ was sent by the Father to suffer and die for the remission of our sins. Christ has died for all, not just for the Christians. However, we must believe on Him. The trinity doctrine has tainted the teachings of Christ and the preaching of the apostles. The people of different faiths could have converted to Christianity if the doctrine of trinity was not invented and introduced by man. This doctrine has given Christianity the flavor of the multi-gods religion that was practiced during the era of the Roman empire. The people who are preaching this man-made trinity doctrine will receive the curse mentioned in Galatians 1:8. Also, these preachers will get a stricter judgment on judgment day, as declared in the New Testament under the Epistle of James 3:1. Christ has said, in Mathew 7:24, if one hears His words and does them, then that person is a wise man who has built his house on a rock; whereas the others on sand.

God gave you an intellect that you should use; otherwise, it is a sin. You cannot blindly follow rituals that have been passed down from generation to generation and shadow a doctrine that contradicts the essence of the old scriptures and the New Testament and dub this action "faith". Christ, in Matthew 25;14-30, narrated a parable about one of the servants who did not use his ability and hid his one 'talents'. The servant was casted out into darkness.

The Council of Nicea has violated the teachings of Christ and the apostles as passed in the New Testament. The defenders of the trinity doctrine were venerated as saints in the churches; however, in my self-effacing mind, I consider these defenders as betrayers of God and His Christ. The collusion they had with the Roman empire has drawn resemblance to Judas who betrayed Christ. On judgment day, we will know how these bishops will fare!

ABOUT THE AUTHOR

I was born in Aram where Christ feet has touched and where He taught. Notwithstanding that I spent 4 years in the seminary, I do not consider myself a theologian, but an engineer. In my younger days, I was not pious because the doctrine of trinity did not dovetail with the New Testament. Later in life, God has touched my life and began to dream of things yet to happen. God works in mysterious ways and I am an instrument to wake up the chosen ones because the return of Christ is in the offing.

Printed in the United States
By Bookmasters